The Sinners' lawyer

The Sinners' lawyer

ALDIVAN TORRES

Canary Of Joy

Contents

1

The Sinners' lawyer
Aldivan Torres
The Sinners' lawyer

Author: Aldivan Torres
2020- Aldivan Torres
All rights reserved.

This book, including all its parts, is copyrighted and cannot be reproduced without the permission of the author, resold or transferred.

Aldivan Torres, born in Brazil, is a writer consolidated in several genres. To date, it has published titles in dozens of languages. From an early age, he was always a lover of the art of writing, having consolidated a professional career from the second half of 2013. He hopes with his writings to contribute to the Brazilian culture, awakening the pleasure of reading in those who do not yet have the habit. Your mission is to win the hearts of each of your readers. In addition to literature, his main tastes are music, travel, friends, family, and the pleasure of living. "For literature, equality, fraternity, justice, dignity, and honor of the human being always" is its motto.

Our Lady of Bonate
The place

The psychic
The appearances
First appearance
Second appearance
Third appearance
Fourth apparition
Fifth apparition
Sixth apparition
Seventh appearance
Eighth appearance
Ninth apparition
Tenth appearance
Tenth first appearance
Tenth-second appearance
Third appearance
Post-appearances
Our Lady of all nations
A little about the psychic
Request from the Queen of Heaven
Main messages
Mediator of all graces
First appearance
Second appearance
Message from the third appearance
Our Lady, Queen of Turzovca
The Miracle Fountain of Okruhla
Virgin of Cuapa
The first appearance
The second appearance
The third appearance
The fourth appearance
The fifth appearance
Our Lady Queen and messenger of peace
Main messages in Jacareí

Our Immaculate Lady Appeared Conception
Main messages on the reserve
Special chapter
Under a tree
In the lottery house
In the crowd
Personal miracles

Our Lady of Bonate

Ghiaie di Bonate-Italy-1944

The place

Ghiaei di Bonate belongs to Diocese de Bergamo, within ten kilometers of the capital. The place is named after the bright ground of the Brembo River. At the time, it was an extremely dangerous place because of bombing in World War II.

In this time of distress and uncertainty, our Lady appears to a seven-year-old girl, bringing a message of peace and hope to the world.

The psychic

In Torchio, Ghiae di Bonate, resided the Roncalli family composed by ten members. It was a humble family, but emotionally stabilized with the creation of children based on Christian values. Example for the children, father, and mother devoted to their work to giving children the minimal survival conditions. While his father worked as a worker at a factory, his mother did handiwork and domestic services. Besides, they supply their young with affection and attention in their spare hours. So, they were admired by everyone who knew them. Your seven daughters and a son were happy.

Adelaide was one of the daughters and at that time she was seven. I was a first-year-high school student with exclusive dedication to studies. She was behaved, polite, kind, healthy, loving and understanding with everyone around her. Completely simple, it was not crossed by his head being chosen by the mother of God as a spokesman of his messages to a world at war, making his name important and famous all over the world.

The appearances
First appearance

May 13, 1944

It's morning. It was Saturday, promising to be within normal. After getting up, shower and eating breakfast, Adelaide met with her brothers and friends on the terrace of her house, spending time with no greater concerns. In these moments of distraction, complicity and harmony she felt exactly the taste of childhood and friendship.

In the afternoon and night period, lunch, reads a book, cleans, listens to the radio and dinner. At 18 hours, I leave the house, obeying the mother's request to collect flowers from Sabugueira and daisy. Your parent loved having flowers decorating the entrance of the house.

When you stand before the image of the Lady, behold, the very thought of her to appear. The beautiful woman wore a whole white set, had a blue robe, a silver crown on her head and a third hanging on her right arm. The woman walked towards the psychic accompanied by two men later recognized as Jose and Jesus. When he got closer, he got in touch:

Don't run away because I'm Our Lady! You must be good, obedient, respectful to the next and sincere. Pray well and come back here for nine nights, always at this hour.

Then it disappeared like smoke. The girl was astonished and scared. He returned because he went home to tell his family that was even more impressed. God's things are really inexplicable.

Second appearance

May 14th, 1944

Adelaide and her friends were concentrating on prayer before the oratory. It was a daily exercise, very profitable and pleasant according to God. Through this effort, they could achieve enough conversions and miracles for the Holy Virgin to be more impudent in the region.

At some point, the psychic felt intimately moved to return to the site of the first appearance of the miraculous saint. What is it? At that moment, nothing suspected of the reasons of it. I would just follow the voice of your intuition with certainty that you were going the right way. This self-confidence was the fruit of his entire trust in the illuminated lady.

In order not to go alone, he called in some hasty, anxious colleagues. Why did you feel that way even though you had a previous experience already consolidated? The plausible explanation was his entirely sensitive to supernatural emotions. Pulling like a cat, she and her companions travel far away quickly. The rush is so much that they can barely see the light sun, the white clouds walking in the sky, the strong, persistent wind hitting their shoulders with a thin voice calling them from afar.

The air of mystery was completely involved in the expedition. The breaking happens when it reaches the desired point. What do they see? Looking up, watching two white dove's passes. A little higher, a bright convoy approaches at high speed, similar to the figure of the sacred family. The group gets expectant. From within the prospect, the image of the Queen of Heaven, as beautiful as the last time. When she gets closer, she asks:

"You must be good, obedient, sincere, pray well and be respectful to the next. Between your 14 and 15, you will become Mother sacramental. You'll suffer a lot, but don't be discouraged because then you'll come with me to Paradise.

When you said that, you opened your arms and blessed her. It went up until it went completely up on the horizon, leaving a trail of sadness and missed. How nice it was to be before the Holy Mother, participating in such special moments. According to the agreement, the girls started the quietest way back. Halfway there, they found a friend who forcefully set off a stop.

"Where were you girls? He asked the boy.

"We came from the country. We just saw Our Lady! Has claimed Adelaide.

"Go back there yet to see if she appears again and ask if I can be a priest consecrating my life to her — He agreed to Adelaide.

As the psychic stepped away, they rested in the middle of the road, enjoying idle time to chat a little. Adelaide was a truly admirable, kind, helpful companion. There was no better person to be chosen by the mother of God to be his confidante on earth. The proof of that was his social engagement for the next and his intense delivery to the Christian Apollo. Everyone was proud of her.

To concentrate on her goal, the servant walked quickly along those royal roads. Not even fatigue was a prevention for you to keep your promise. His joy was precisely the fact that he served each other. Noticed, a virtue to be praised and blessed by God.

When he reached the scene of appearances, he raised his eyes to the heavens, waiting with faith a divine manifestation. After a few minutes of waiting, your prayers were answered. Like lightning, on your side, your ready lawyer appeared.

"Yes, he will be a Missionary Priest according to the Holy Heart, when the war ended, revealed the venerable Mary.

With the mission accomplished, this vision went away slowly. The maid has retained her journey by going to meet her colleagues. He told them what he heard, and the boy's joy was complete. Together, they returned to their respective abode. There was still more to do during the day with God's blessing.

Third appearance

May 15th, 1944

The servant of God was in the same place as the other appearances, exercising his religious gift. Each of these moments was considered sacred for her feeling happy, fulfilled and filled with endless peace. Undisguisable, this was an achievement attributed to the sacred Queen of Heaven.

Instantly, a bright point and two white doves approach the scene. Surely, there was something supernatural about this, this venerable madam concentrated his attentions on the objects approaching at an astonishing speed. From within the light, she can behold the mystery of the sacred family. She can see clearly the figures of Jesus and Mary's well-dressed, bright, featured features, imposing and decisive ports. That's when she started contact.

"Please, my mother, I ask you for the cure of the people who seek you and I also request peace with the consequent end of the war.

"Tell them if they want their children to be cured, they must pray hard and avoid certain sins. If men do penance, the war will end between two months, otherwise in just under two years.

"Then let's start praying while we have time.

"Yes. I'll help you.

The two accomplices prayed together, a part of the third. Slowly, the image of the sacred family was disappearing. Now, the little maid would seek to divulge among the acquaintances and practice the advice given by her master. There was still time to save the world from total destruction.

Fourth apparition

May 16, 1944

Last night and our dear friend came back to the same point. Directly, the bright point and the doves came back to appear with the manifestation of Jesus, Jose, and Mary. The Holy Virgin opened a wide smile and drastically changing her features to sadness said:

"So many mothers have children unhappy for their grave sins. Don't make any more sins and the children will heal.

"I want a signal coming from you to satisfy people's desire.

"This will happen in time too. Pray for the poor sinners who need children's prayers.

Watching the horizon, the Immaculate sighed and rising according to the devotee. One more step had been successfully fulfilled before God and the world.

Fifth apparition

May 17, 1944

Fulfilled her duties of the day, our sister in Christ has gone again to the site of appearances, waiting for another date. It didn't take long and the bright spot appears, Our Lady and eight angels. She's willing to contact her.

"I came to trust you with a secret. In a while, peace will return to Earth with the presence of my divine son restored the union between men. It shall be born in Brazil within a reality of miserable facing the greatest prejudices in society. He's coming to bring the light!

"How and when?

"Still cannot be revealed. Come on! Tell the bishop and the pope the secret, I trust you… I recommend you do what I said, but not tell anyone else.

"All right!

"Be at peace!

The appearance was slowly disappearing, and the psychic began to cry with emotion and happiness for the world to have been graced with another gift from God. Coming home, completed your prayers and went to sleep.

Sixth apparition

May 18, 1944

At the usual place, our lady appeared along with two doves and angels around her. Sitting slowly said:

"Prayer and penance. Pray for the most obstinate sinners who are dying at this moment and that they hurt my heart.

"Okay. I will. What prayer do you like most?

"The prayer I like most is the Hail Mary.

Then the vision disappeared. As a way to honor her, the psychic sang chants in her honor. It was always nice to thank you for everything that was going on at that place.

Seventh appearance

May 19, 1944

In the place of prayers, the servant beholds the mystery of the sacred family in another of their appearances. You saw Jesus, Mary, and Joseph completely united and dressed in the light. Besides these, he saw angels around him. How beautiful God's things were in his rich details. I still wasn't believing that I had the honor of seeing such things.

"Our Lady, people have asked me to ask if the sick children must be brought here, so they can heal.

"No, there's no need for everyone to come here. Those who can, come. According to your sacrifices, you will be healed, or you will remain ill, but do no more grave sins.

"Can you work some miracle, so people can believe?

"This will happen, many will convert, and I will be recognized by the Church. Meditating in these words every day of your life. Have courage in all the difficulties. You'll see me at the time of your death, I'll put you under my robe and take you to heaven.

A smoke filled the environment and the mother of God's mother's vulnerability is gone. Very cheerful on the promise of the saint, Adelaide went to rest, thinking of all recent facts. His faith in God grew more and more and more was a fact to be celebrated.

Eighth appearance

May 20, 1944

On top of the Stone, the divine maid struggled in her prayers, waiting for another supernatural event. By attending his pleads, the sacred family has come to him again, united by the cause.

"Tomorrow will be the last time I speak to you, then for seven days I'll let you think straight about what I told you. You just try to understand because when you're bigger, it'll do you a lot if you want to be all mine. After these seven days I'll come back four times, you've claimed Our Lady.

"But will you leave me, my mother?

"Never. In my heart, there will always be a captive place for you. I'll be at your spiritually side, suggesting good deeds.

"Good. I'm watching your messages and getting as much out of the people as possible.

"Very well. Keep doing that, especially for the poor sinners. There are many people lost because there are no sacrifices or asks for them.

"There's a certain ally in me.

"I know that. May God cover you with blessings!

Changing the direction of the eye, the soul of the queen of heaven has set on its way to heaven. The mission of the day was, so to speak, accomplished.

Ninth apparition

May 21, 1944

The same two doves appear as always announcing the manifestation of the sacred family being in the middle of the Church. Four animals found themselves before the main door, a gray donkey, a white sheep, a white dog and a brown horse. On your knees, animals prayed. Among them, the horse stood up and moved to the lily field, where he trampled them with perversity. Jose followed him and avoided any major damage. Then he returned to the church door to resume prayers. In the matter in question, the horse represents the head of a family or religious faction. Far from his business, causes ruin and disorder. As we go back to acting, things are headed to success aided by magnitude, faith, and attitude represented by other animals.

Tenth appearance

May 28, 1944

It was the day of the first communion of that devoted servant of Mary. It was a singular moment to give your heart to God. More than ever, now I understood the meaning of his mission: to fight for peace and conversion of the poor sinners.

Coming home, he met at the same time and time as before, presenting his sincere offers. That's when the bright spot brought with him the mother of God and two saints, St. Lucas and St. Judas.

"Pray for the obstinate sinners who make my heart suffer because they don't think of death. Pray for the Holy Father who goes through a bad time. So many abuses him and many attempt on his life. I'll protect him, and he won't leave the Vatican. Peace won't take long, but my heart waits for that world peace in which everyone loves each other as brothers. Only then will the Pope suffer less, recommended our Holy Mother.

Mary's look brought serenity and compassion for the mistakes of her servant. On his side, two black doves symbolized the family's union and her support for all mankind. With all these elements, the apostle felt safe to follow with her dreams and purposes. I did this in honor of the Holy Mother and of our Lord Jesus Christ. Relax, the redeemer was moving away little by little until it disappeared completely. At the moment, Adelaide had rested from her work with much more optimism and hope than once. Mercy had won justice.

Tenth first appearance

May 29th, 1944

On this day, our Lady with angels in a red dress. In his hands, he carried the two black doves and, on his arm, he was hanging the third. Opening a light smile, the queen of the heavens said:

"The sick who wants to heal must have greater confidence and sanctify their sufferings if they want to go to heaven. If you don't, you'll get no prize and be severely punished. I hope all those who know my word make all the efforts to deserve heaven. Those who suffer without regret will obtain from me and my son all they ask. Pray for those who have the sick soul. My son Jesus died at the Cross to save everyone. Many people don't understand these words, and that's why I suffer.

"Yes, I will continue with my prayers in favor of the poor sinners, assured the devout.

"Good! I'm happy for them!

By sending a kiss, the Holy Virgin has been distanced away from the angels and the doves. Alone, our sister in Christ was seeking internal solutions for her fears and yet unrealized projects. The only thing he had left was faith in Our Lady, and that was enough for himself.

Tenth-second appearance

May 30, 1944

It seemed to be a day like any other day until the exact moment when the pitying manifested again along with angels flying from one side to another. Brilliant as light and dressed with admirable taste, reflected its noblest intentions through the pink dress and the white veil. After a brief breath, he communicated:

"Dear girl, you are all mine, but even though you are in my heart tomorrow, tomorrow I will leave you in this valley of tears and pain. You will see me at the time of your death and wrapped in my veil I will lead you to heaven. With you, there will be all those who understand and suffer.

"Already? What will become of me without my protector?

"What does it say? I would never have the courage to abandon her. I will be present at all times suggesting good deeds, comforting your pain, victories, and defeats. But I'll be invisible. It's reasonable to understand that I don't belong in this world, and therefore you won't be able to see me anymore.

"I understand, even with the sad heart. Give me strength, my mother.

"I'll be with you always! A higher force calls me. See you next time!

"See you later.

Alone, the Christian had no choice but to rest, thinking of all those facts so revealing and heavy. It hadn't come to an end yet.

Third appearance

May 31, 1944

It's dawn. The new day brought emotions and actions impregnated with a feeling of farewell. Our dear psychic kept thinking of her religious, the reasons for her mission, the people who accompanied her, the faith in God and herself and her freedom.

As a good citizen, he was performing exemplarily his tasks, carrying an invisible painful weight. It was like they wanted to rip a piece of their heart out and leave it without feelings or soul. More than anything, he felt like a person from heaven due to their values, beliefs, actions, works, and goodness. His immediate desire was to fly to heaven and live with Jesus and his beloved mother. Is that selfish of you? Unlike what she thought, God would use it as a divine instrument of reconciliation with humanity involved in dense darkness. Her life, as well as other consecrations, were, for, a milestone.

At dusk, he gathered mercy at the usual place. A very intense vigil was followed by, where her worshiped entity appeared around twenty hours. Your appearance has turned out exactly like the first time with a happier, seriously, decided and firm look.

"My dear little girl, I'm sorry to have to leave you, but my time has passed. Don't be scared if you won't see me for a while. Think about what I told you, at the time of your death I'll come again. In this valley of pain, you will be a small martyr. Don't lose your nerve. I wish my triumph soon. Pray for the Pope and tell him to do it quickly because I want to be zealous to everyone in this place. Anything I'm asked of; I'll intercede with my son. I'll be your reward if your martyrdom is merry. These words will serve you as comfort in ordeal. Support everything with patience and come with me to heaven. Those who will willingly make you suffer, will not go to heaven if they have not fixed everything and deeply regret. Be happy, for we shall see you yet, my little martyr.

"Oh, how I feel and rejoice at the same time! Go in peace, my holy mother. I appreciate this time together and consequent learning. I will not rest in my prayers to win the world.

"You've certainly won! Just keep faith in my divine son and me. Pray for sinners and deceivers!

"Yes! Together, we shall win the darkness.

"Amen. Be at peace.

Our lady gave her a soft kiss on her face and the tears kept falling from the Servant. Slowly, the figure of God's mother was drifting away with the certainty of one more cycle fulfilled. Soon she'd come back to help her beloved children all over the earth. Long live the Holy Mother of God.

Post-appearances

The news of the appearances soon spread to make the little young lady a celebrity. Consequently, it has aroused a lot of envy of some Christian currents. She became the target of a pursuit, and having so little experience ended up putting her in contradiction in front of the facts.

The worst scenario was drawing. You were practically forced to sign a negative term on appearances, weighing considerably in the recognition process of the facts reported. Undefeated, she tried to move on to the religious life by entering the convent when she turned 15. Again, the forces of darkness have harmed you, what resulted in your expulsion from the institution.

Still, the young lady didn't let herself get down. He married and moved to Milan where he looked after the poor, sick, orphans, and widows being a true Christian example. In truth, no force on earth would be able to stop you from happiness. Further, further, he reaffirmed the facts that happened before the authorities. The world would have to know Mary's ready disposition to help her children, and she was living proof of it.

Our Lady of all nations
Amsterdam-Holland (1945-1972)

A little about the psychic

Born August 13th, 1905, in Alkmaar in Holland, Ida Peerdeman was the youngest of five brothers. From birth, childhood, and youth that she demonstrated a lovely human sensitivity to other people. Besides, she was polite, responsible, hard-working, loving, religious and exercised the practice of good. No wonder, she was chosen by our Heaven mother to be her spokesman among men. There were several appearances in the long years and to not stretch too much we'll go to the main points of this event.

Request from the Queen of Heaven

"Lord Jesus Christ, Son of the Father, send thy spirit upon the earth. It makes the Holy Spirit inhabits in the hearts of all people, to be preserved of corruption, of calamity and war. May the Lady of all the people, who once was MARY, be our lawyer. Amen.

"That she be treated by mankind as a corridor, mediator, lawyer, path, example and brotherly mother.

"Your title regarding this appearance would be: "Lady of all people."

"The cross must be the greatest symbol of Christianity in every way.

"Practice and spread the devotion of the Rosario incessantly.

"Let people do penance, analyze their failures, correct them with the firm resolution of change for the better.

"Let the ecclesiastic set a good example so that their fruits are visible to all. In fact, good fruit comes from only good trees.

"There's no other way to fight evil but through good. Christians must unite around the blessed cross and their compassionate mother in order that they may defeat evil.

"Men must seek a relationship with a complete, transparent and worthy God. Follow the commandments and divine laws in particular that sums all others, love God over all things, to the next as yourself.

"Show an effective performance as an apostle of good through the pillars: justice, love, mercy, charity, sympathy, bonanza, faith, tolerance, tolerance, equality.

Main messages

"Don't ask for signs. This is a temptation. There's no greater proof than my words.

"It's time for the Holy Spirit to come over all mankind.

"Hard times come upon the face of the earth. Time of restlessness, turbulence, lies, perversion, subversion, disbelief, pursuit of Christians and people wanting to rule the world.

"Corruption is the one who causes the decay of the world.

"Men haven't realized how bad the world is.

"They want to annihilate religions in a way that no one will notice.

"The evil is spreading all over the world.

"There are many false prophets who instead of helping the Christ are serving the purposes of Satan.

"More and more, Satan corrupts the world with his seductions.

"People are more concerned about material things, their salvation.

"Youth lacks guidance and stimulation, so they grow good values and follow an idiotic religious life.

"Mary was sent by the Lord of the armies to help her children. That's why it's called "Lady of all people".

"In front of God and Mary, the faithful join with the certainty of God and, resulting in heavenly protection.

"Christians must unite around the figure of Jesus Christ, for he is the only one who can save.

"More than guidance, young people need your help and understanding.

"The goal of appearances is to warn sinners to emerge, get forgiveness of sins and save themselves.

"Only by giving yourself to the Messiah is possible that we can achieve peace.

"Believe in God and in his son, and then peace will remain with you.

"I did penance for the world. That way, salvation will come.

"The divine laws and its updates are worth every time as if they were new.

"The father and son sent Mary as correspondent, mediator, lawyer, and mother of all mankind.

"The people of the world will not find peace until they submit to the cross.

You choose the weakest and pure for the greater missions.

Mediator of all graces

Marienfried-Germany-1946

First appearance

April 25th, 1946

There's thunder, then Mary appears like lightning in front of psychic Barbara Reuss. With a sad, complacent look, the contact began.

"There was the greatest trust is and where the men I can do everything, and I will spread peace. After all men believe in my power, peace will reign. I am the sign of God alive. I print my signal on the front of my children. The star will pursue him, but he will beat the star.

"Who are you? Asked the young woman.

"If I didn't have this veil, you'd recognize me. I'm the mediator of all grace.

"Right! What do you want?

"I've come to pass the peace of Christ.

"Why do you perform sad?

"My kids are forgetting me. That's why I'm grieving.

"What are the consequences of that?

"You won't be able to reach before God.

"What can we do then?

"Pray for all sinners. Acting like this, my grace will remain with you at all times.

"I'll do it! Thank you!

"I'm glad. Now I have to go. God be with you.

"Amen.

The beautiful lady changed the look and went up next. The first part of the mission was so to speak complete.

Second appearance

May 25th, 1946

In the same place as always, divine providence was manifested again. The looks of the two women crossed at a time of total complicity. There was something to be said between them.

"I'm the great Mediator of Grace. The same way the world can't find Mercy next to the father, except for the sacrifice of the son, so you cannot be heard by my son, except through my intercession. CHRIST is little known because I'm not known. The Father spilled the chalice of his wrath upon the peoples because these refused his son. The world was consecrated to my Immaculate Heart, but this consecration has become many a terrible responsibility. I ask the world to live this consecration. You have unlimited confidence in my Immaculate Heart. Believe me. I can all along with my son. Put in place of your heart stained by sin, my Immaculate Heart, and then I will be. I will draw the strength of God, and Father's love will again reproduce you to the perfect image of CHRIST. Hear my request in order that I may soon reign as King of Peace. Pray and sacrifice thee for sinners. I offered, by my intermedius, to you, and all your action to the father. Put you at my disposal. Pray the Rosario. Don't just request material goods. Now it's about praying for something worth a lot more. Don't expect miracles. I want to act hidden as the great Mediator of Grace. It is the peace of the heart that I wish you to grant, if you do as I ask.

That said, the virgin smiled and disappeared. Alone, the servant gathered the elements obtained and linked them to her personal mission. There was still time to act for the world.

Message from the third appearance

June 25th, 1946

"I offered many sacrifices. I have made your prayer a sacrifice. Don't be selfish. What it's worth is this: offering Eternal Gloria and atonement. If you are completely at my disposal, at all, I will arrange it. I will carry my beloved sons of heavy crosses because I love him in my immolate son. I ask you, be ready to carry the cross, to come to peace soon.

Our Lady, Queen of Turzovca

Slovakia-1958

Matus was a ranger. Raised without a mother, learned the basis of Christianity by himself and decided to follow it. He was a simple, fearful, faithful man in God and in Our Lady.

On June 1, 1958, Matos was doing the routine rounds in Okruhla, a saw near Turzovka. Besides the work itself, he loved to walk, listen to the birds' singing, feel the heat of the sun and the cold breeze hitting his face. Along with nature, he felt closer to the divine. As soon as he reached the side of the mountain named Zivcak, he took the chance to pray before the image of Our Lady of Perpetual Help under a pine tree.

He began the prayers of our Father-in-law and the Hail Mary. But before it was finished, it was surprised by a divine demonstration. Like it was a flash of light, the image of a woman appeared floating in front of him. The beautiful figure had her hands bent and wore a glowing crown. His hair was long, he wore a blue strap and next to his feet were scented roses. On his right arm, he carried a rosary.

You walked a little and Matus followed her. In a field of white roses, the fence was damaged. The woman pointed towards a hammer and nails. The psychic then understood that he should fix it. Hours on wire, he worked on this job. By concluding it, the lady showed one of her most beautiful smiles. Extending his arm, the servant touched the rosary and instantly felt the urge to practice that devotion, even though he didn't even know it.

The lady changed the direction of her look into the tree where her image was sheltered. In it, the psychic can see a screen showing the world's territories. With countries represented by various colors, green meant "Nice to God" and yellow represented deserter nations. In a moment, the world seemed to be burning. That's when the following message came up: "Repent thee! Pray for priests and religious! Pray the Rosario!

Matus got scared, and then he looked at his lady. In turn, she asked him to observe a little above her. That's when a bang happened and the sky cleared as lightning from the heavens the figure of Christ himself. He came with majesty and authority. He wore a white robe and a red cape. On the left side, he carried a cross and could clearly see his sacred heart to the center of his chest, punished by human sins. From inside, three resuscitating rays were coming out. Stunned by so many emotions, the guard passed out.

A few minutes later, I woke up due to the strong sound of bells coming from the nearest church because it was Angeles's time. He sat down, thinking about all the facts for a few moments. Instinctively, he took the rosary left by the lady and put himself to pray, inspired by a greater force. When this exercise was finished, it all seemed clearer as his own transcribed statement below, "After the appearance, I felt a great infusion of faith. First, I had to make peace with the people I had conflicted with me. I wish I could have avoided that, but I felt like I had to do it. After returning from the mountain that same night, I went to beg the forgiveness of all the people in Turzovka and the surrounding area. I did it as if against my own will. And it took me late at night. People were surprised, some laughed at me, others thought I'd gone mad. The next day, in the morning, I made a confession and went to communion. From that moment on, I was cured of all my illnesses. First, the heavy cough I had and that bothered me for many years and that the doctors said it was incurable."

After this day, there were six more appearances from Our Lady to the psychic. Each vision has brought an important message to mankind. With the disclosure of the facts, many envied his condition and orchestrated him a betrayal. He ended up being arrested by the Communists and thought of as crazy. In the psychiatric hospital, he suffered electrocution, hypnotism, chemical cure and constant interrogations. However, his faith in God and our Lady remained intact.

The Miracle Fountain of Okruhla

A man named Jaroslav Zaalenka had a dream about a beautiful woman asking you to go to the mountain of Okruha and Dig. After three days, he went to fulfill this request. Up the steep trails of the place, he wondered if he was in perfect sense for following the recommendation of a dream. It was a painful, tiring climb, and it would have to be worth it.

When he reached the top, he chose a rocky spot to dig. Soon at first, the beautiful lady appeared to you in the right location, disappearing right after. Your work was rewarding with the discovery of a clear water source. Word spread and the people who took from the water were instantly cured of their evils. Cures of lung cancer, blindness, paralysis among others. It's been conceived, for the following prophecy: "In a few years, you'll have another Lourdes in Slovakia, where you go on pilgrimage."

Virgin of Cuapa

Cuapa-Nicaragua-1980

Bernardo Martinez was in charge of the Cuapa chapel. From March 1980, strange counsels began to happen around you. Let's face it, for many times, this servant of God found lights on in the chapel and once again saw the image of the saint illuminated. By investigating the cases, he found no plausible explanation for the same. That's when it got even more confusing, with several assumptions going through your mind.

One day, he told some people what happened to him, asking for discretion. That was for nothing because soon many people knew the fact. The news reached the ears of the city's priest, who was interested in history and went to meet with him to solve some questions.

"Is it true what they said about the demonstrations here in the Church?

"Yes. It's all true, Father.

"Tell me everything.

"For many times, I found lights on in the church with no explanation. Another time, I saw the image of the saint enlightened.

"Okay. What do you pray for?

"The rosary and three Hail Mary. Since I was a child, my grandmother taught me to be devoted to the Lady.

"Can you ask the virgin what she wants from us? What if it can be clearly manifested?

"I can try.

"Thank you. My prayers will be with you, son.

"Thank you.

"Now I have to go. Any news, let me know.

"Yes.

The priest returned to the city to fulfill his duties while the psychic was thinking about his request. How would you do it now? The last thing I wanted was complications. So, as soon as you could pray like this:

"Holy Mother, please don't ask for anything from me. I have many problems in church. Make your requests to someone else because I want to avoid any more trouble. I have a lot of them at the moment. I don't want any more.

It's been a little while and the story about the image has been forgotten. As for Bernardo, he kept on in his daily prayers. Interestingly, the Holy Virgin prepared her for her mission to be spokesperson for her messages.

The first appearance

It was early May. In that time, Bernardo was facing an internal crisis due to lack of money, professional, religious and spiritual problems. All this was a strong depression and in consequence, it lacked motivation to perform the capricious activities of day to day. Lived a dark night, wicked dark, dark night without the perspective of immediate solutions.

On second thought, his spirit requested a cry of freedom. The only way out to his mind was to walk and fish in the river because it was always a pleasant and relaxing activity for him. So, you did. He got up early carrying a bag and a machete. On the way, his thought was connected with nature and with the sensations that were caused. Everything was really invigorating and promising, the hot sun, the thin breeze, the rocks of the way looking to speak to him, the thorns, the claws, the trees, the mountain and its adversity. Being on the way there was similar to the task of a young Brazilian dreamer who never gave up his dreams. Even if I didn't realize that, the situation was pretty much the same.

When he got to the river, the distraction was given up. He took a bath, fished and rested in those limpid waters given by God, understanding a little divine mystery. How nice it was to live that misogynous moment. No problem afflicted you at that moment, being credited to a miracle of the Queen of Heaven.

It came in the afternoon and ecstasy was so great that man was not hungry or any needs. Shortly after, it started raining, having him shelter under a tree. Busy, began to pray the rosary. When the weather got better, he went to a hose to eat fruit, cut a branch in the woods and went to other trees to get fruit. By the time you realized, it was three o'clock in the afternoon. At this moment, an anguish traveled through his heart for knowing his duties in the city. What a pity! I was so happy there along the nature, looking like the rest didn't matter at all.

Walking towards another point saw lightning. Was it going to rain? Time was unable to sign that, and it impressed him even more. Further ahead, the phenomenon repeated. On the screen of his mind, the figure of a beautiful, majestic woman appears. Let's see the exact description of the psychic about what happened:

There was a small tree in Norisco over the rocks and over that tree was the cloud, it was extremely white. He'd lightning strikes in every direction, rays of light like the sun. In the cloud were the feet of a beautiful lady. His feet were barefoot. The dress was long and white. She had a heavenly cord around her chest. Long sleeves. Covering it was a veil of a pale cream with gold embroidery on the edges. His hands were laid together on his chest. It looked like the image of the Virgin of Fatima. It was still.

In the face of the unusual, man felt surprised. Thousands of unrelated thoughts were passing through your head pointing out the possible motives of that. Thinking it's a dream, he slaps his face with his hands. But when I removed them, the strange figure remained in the same place to stare at him. So, you convinced yourself of the truth of the facts. Then the woman extended her arms towards her, and she emanated a radius of strong light. The feeling that caused by this action made the psychic perplexed. He felt with an indescribable, confident, and full of happiness never experienced. I needed to because I investigate the facts even before the freezing fear now provoked.

"What's your name?

"Mary.

"Where are you from?

"I came from heaven. I'm Jesus's mother.

"What do you want?

"I want Rosario to be prayed every day.

"Yes, we're praying. The priest brought us the intentions of the parish of San Francisco so that we can join them.

"I want you to be prayed permanently, in the family including children who are old enough to understand, to be prayed at a time when there's no trouble with the work of the house.

"How do you want us to pray?

"You don't like prayers done running or mechanically. Pray the Rosario with the reading of Bible quotes and put in practice the word of God.

"How? Where are the Bible quotes?

"Search the holy book with wisdom. You'll find them.

"What's the highest commandment?

"Love each other. Do your duty.

"Right! My dear queen, how can we reach peace?

"Make peace. Don't ask our Lord for peace because if you don't make it, there will be no peace.

"I get it! How do you get your help and grace?

"Renew the first five Saturdays. You got many thanks when everyone did that.

"Before the war, we used to do that. We were going to confession and communion every first Saturday of the month, but as the Lord had already freed us from bloodshed in Cuapa, we did not continue with this practice.

"Nicaragua has suffered a lot since the earthquake. She's threatened with even more suffering. She'll continue to suffer if you don't change.

Mary took a break. Your serious look changed to a face of sorrow quickly. Then she went on:

"Pray my son, Rosario, all over the world. Tell the believers and not believers that the world is threatened by grave dangers. I asked the Lord to slow down His justice, but if you don't change, you'll rush the arrival of World War III.

"Ma'am, I don't want any trouble; I have many in church. Tell that to someone else.

"Now because our Lord chose him to give the message.

The virgin signaled that she was leaving. That's when the servant remembered something important.

"Madam, don't go because I want to go tell you. Consuelo because she told me she wanted to see her.

"No. Not everyone can see me. She'll see me when I take her to heaven, but she must pray Rosario like I asked. Be at peace! See you next time!

"See you later!

The cloud lifted, and with it took the saint's figure. Alone, the devoted Marian left their, starting his way back to town. It would be a great chance for you to reflect on the advice of the lighting. However, within the interior, I had already made a serious decision, not to tell anyone what you saw and heard there. It showed a little selfishness on his part, but it was also part of an internal protection mechanism. What would the others say? How do you give credit to a simple handler? It was fearsome for your safety to reveal this secret now.

Coming to town, prayed Rosario in the chapel and returned home in complete silence. However, every moment that passed, his conscience weighed and a wave of sorrow came through his heart. Collected in your room in prayer, received the divine message that you should tell. Insistent, he prayed again to Rosario, asking for the enlightenment of the creator father about the facts. At this point, the fear of being chased was greater than the message itself, Maryna.

It's been a while, and he's gone on with his routine. Though he tried to distract himself, nothing was ever funny because he was always that inner voice insisting that he told me about the appearance. It was almost like a good chase. While his stubbornness remained with him trying to appear strong when he actually found himself nearly a nervous attack. How many times have we not acted like him before others or himself? Fear and incomprehension really lock their soul in the worst of chains. He was missing a little maturity or a sign of fate that forced him.

One day, I was walking in the field looking for a calf from his herd. As much as I walked, I couldn't find the animal. He was already desperate when the same previous phenomenon happened before him. The

Queen of Heaven again thought she was present a more serious look than the other time.

"Why didn't you say what I sent you to say?

"Ma'am, I'm afraid. I'm afraid I'm going to be the ridiculous person, afraid that they're going to laugh at me, that they don't believe me. Those who don't believe this will laugh at me. They'll say I'm crazy.

"Don't be afraid. I'll help you, and tell the priest.

"All right!

The appearance went missing in front of him like smoke. Walking further forward, the pastor saw the calf and took him to the river, where he gave him water. Thereafter, he came home. He got ready and went to friends' house. There, you told all the facts. As an answer, you were reprimanded. However, the weight of consciousness has dissipated. Thanks to Mary, he felt free once again.

In the next few days, he started telling people he knew. As expected, some didn't believe he was crazy. But just the fact that you told him was good. That's when he discovered the importance and the core of his mission, to be instrumented to the word divine. As for the challenges, it was necessary to deliver all the problems of disbelief to the Lord's feet, where his power would solve the confusion. There was no reason to doubt the Holy Mother of God in front of evidence so clear.

Days later, the time came to meet with the vicar of the parish. In the Church, he testified about everything he saw and heard about the appearances. At the end of the story, the man of God was reflected and continued:

"Would it be someone who wants to scare you in those hills?

"I don't think so. Until there was a possibility of doing it in the river and in the hills, but in the middle of the pasture, it's not possible for there to be an open field.

"Could it be a temptation that's chasing you?

"I don't know why I could just talk about what I saw and heard.

"Go to the place of appearances and pray Rosario there. When you visualize the appearance, make the sign of the cross. In fact, being good or bad, nothing will get to you.

"All right! Thank you so much for listening to me!

"I'm at your disposal! God bless you!

"Amen!

The pastor walked away from the site, initiating the happiest return home. Finally, the ancient roadblocks had been overcome with praise thanks to the miracles provoked by the saint. With faith in her, I'd go on her way with certain things would work out. Thank you and praise the queen of heaven!

The second appearance

Following the priest's recommendations, the psychic, and some people have returned to the scene of appearances. Once we get there, Rosario was prayed. However, despite all expectations, no phenomenon has occurred. The only way out of the group was to come home totally disappointed. What had happened? For the first time, the devoted Marian saw his forces weaken in public.

The answer to your restlessness came through a night dream. The beautiful lady came forward just after lightning and was physiologically the same as the first appearance.

"What do you want, Mother?

"I want Rosario to be prayed every day.

"I have some requests to make you....

"Some will be attended, some will not. Look at the sky!

Looking in the direction, the psychic can see a group of people dressed in white going into the sun. Resplendent and enlightened, they sang glories to the Lord. It was a gorgeous party. Even from a distance, the viewer could feel all the happiness of the same. Our Lady then explained:

"See, these are the first communities when Christianity began. They're the first catechists; many of them were martyrs. Do you want to be martyrs? Do you want to be a martyr yourself?

Even without the dimension of what that proposal represented, the servant of God answered yes. Due to his acceptance, a new image presented itself, another numerous group also dressed in white color. They carried luminous rosaries between their hands and one of them a book. While one was reading messages, the others were reflecting for a few moments. Then they prayed to our Father-Our and ten Hail Mary's. All the gifts prayed together what gave that prayer a fantastic power. At the end of this activity, the conversation continued.

"These are the first ones I gave Rosario to. That's the way I wish you all to pray for Rosario.

"Yes. We'll pray like this.

Another vision has happened. Similar to the Franciscans, carried each of their Rosario in prayer. At the end of their passage, the virgin said:

"These received Rosario from the hands of the first.

The visions followed on the screen of the servant's mind. What was now presented was a gigantic procession of all races, colors and ethnics. The Rosario was a common piece to be carried by them, showing the strength of the Lady. Each one reflected the divine light.

"Ma'am, I'm going with these because they're dressed like me.

"No. You're still in short. You must tell people what you've been seeing and hearing.

"All right!

"I have shown you the glory of our Lord and you will have it if you are obedient to our Lord, the Word of the Lord, if you persevere in the Holy Rosario's prayer and put in practice the Word of the Lord.

The vision disappeared, and then the handler woke up. The other day, he met with the priest, telling him everything. For guidance of it, you kept a secret regarding these facts. A few days later, the permission was given to him and then some people in the village heard about it. The entrance was pretty receptive. Another miracle attributed to the Holy Virgin.

The third appearance

The psychic and about forty people returned to the scene of appearances. It was a unique and special moment where they sang, glorified and prayed to God. While the strange lady left them silently, frustrating again the expectations of everyone. He was left as an alternative to the pilgrims to return home.

In the quiet of his home, the pastor gathered in his room, soon asleep due to his tired. In his night passages, he came in the same dream-shaped messages, he was at the same location as praying around the world. Following the master's recommendations, he was intensely dedicated to Rosario in favor of the Christian religious. During the act, he remembered the sister of a prisoner who had requested his intercession. You decided because you also prayed for him.

The servant knelt as a reverence and raised his hands, begging for the boy. In a moment, when changing the direction of the look, saw an angel near the rocks. He was young, tall, thin and wearing all white clothes.

"Your prayer was heard, the angel said.

The prophet's heart jumped with joy. What do you mean you're heard? He was aware of the power of his intercessions, but that case was truly difficult. So, surprise her.

"Go and tell the prisoner's sister to go and console him on Sunday because he's too sad to advise him not to sign a document, which will press him to sign a paper on which he takes responsibility for a sum of money; he's innocent. Tell her she shouldn't worry; she'll be able to talk to him alone for a long time; that she'll be treated in a friendly way. Tell him to go Monday to the Judigalpa Police Headquarters to complete every step to his release because he'll be released that day. Tell him to take 1,000 cordobas because they'll set bail -continued the angel.

"I have two orders from a cousin to make for the Holy Virgin. The requests are related to problems because of the addiction of father and brother's drinking and trouble at work.

"People around them must be patient with them, and they shouldn't complain when they're intoxicated.

"All right! I'll pass this message on.

"Go and tell them to stop addiction, to do it little by little and that way desire will leave you.

"Roger that. This is an excellent strategy.

"Tell your cousin he'll be mugged and get shot in the foot, precisely on the left heel. Time after that, they'll kill him.

"This sentence on my cousin cannot be revoked by the prayer of several Rosario?

"No. That's how he'll die, but if he hears your advice, his life can be prolonged.

"What about my cousin's work?

"She shouldn't be afraid. You must stay strong as you are. You mustn't leave your job because as a teacher who has faith in Our Lord, she can do people a lot of good.

"Right! How am I supposed to behave in front of these events?

"Don't turn your back on your problems and curse no one.

That said, the angel disappeared. At the same time, the psychic woke up. It was morning and the sun's heat waves crossed the cracks of the house, coming to him. It made him feel totally renewed and ready for the surprises of the new day.

With an open smile, he rises, moving from his room to the bathroom. There, in your intimacy, you talk to yourself by starting body and soul cleaning. For some, undressing and washing was just a social convection. For him, it was a ritual of communion with God and his nature. At that exact moment, there was no reason to lie or deceive yourself about your mission being so important. It was time to reflect, analyze the flaws and trace the future with the certainty that God was in charge of everything. In this one, I could blindly trust because I never left him alone when I needed him most. It was because, grateful for that and in return, he was struggling for being a good Christian.

The results of what we exampled above showed in his actions what caused the admiration of others. Because you were a model, you couldn't let down your blood. Decided to trust the cousin of the secret passed by the angel, although it was at risk of being considered a madman. However, his only way out was to risk it.

I'm sure he conducts the cleaning session with relative tranquility. Exercise recovers your optimism, mental health and disposition. At the end of the stage, I was ready to face the constant challenges that life had imposed you. There was no doubt that I was able to overcome them.

Coming out of the shower, goes back to the room where you dry, you wear the clean clothes, you comb your hair, you wear your favorite perfume and analyze your profile in the mirror. You'd have to be impeccable targeting successive events. The same promised to be quite enlightening.

When it's done, you go to the kitchen where you prepare and eat a quick snack. Satisfied, you leave the house, and you go to meet two people, the prisoner's brother and Mrs. Help. Trust them your secret. Even reluctant, they promise to follow the instructions given by the angel through the dream.

On Sunday, they went to visit the recluse. Your cousin can be alone with the prisoner for a long time to ask you not to sign any papers. When he returned to Cuapa, he requested a loan.

On Monday, as announced by the angel, he was released from the bail. In thanks to the warning, Rosario was prayed. This news has spread across the region, giving a greater credibility to this series of appearances. It was like a reward for their effort.

Giving proceedings to the requests received in the vision, the psychic talked to his uncle and cousin. The first believed in the message promising to leave the drinking addiction. The second one made a little of advice. Time was passing and the angel's predictions came true. However, the heart of some remained hardened. It proves God's love even in the face of man's indifference and cold.

Days later, the time had come to meet with Our Lady. At the agreed time, the psychic, and his group moved to the point of appearances. However, they gave up due to the difficulty of crossing the river because it was full. What a pity! The rains and current winds which were the reasons of the phenomenon in the river helped the environment and the country man. But they stopped a liberating date. That's why they were so sorry about you and contradictions satisfied by heavenly help. These two opposites complement each other and caused a divine miracle.

As an option for them not to miss the tour, the Christians spread around the rocks on the river shores. In one voice, they prayed to Rosario and praised the Lord through new chants. At this intermission, the volume of water from the river has slowed down a little, what made the group cross. However, the beautiful lady didn't show up, causing frustration on some of them. At that moment, they would have to understand that God's time was not the same as theirs. So, the only plausible exit was to go home, and that's precisely what they did.

With the seventh failures to see the Holy Virgin, disbelief has taken over some. Among them, was the vicar of the parish. However, he has been willing to go to the apparition's site to find out more deeply the facts. And so it happened. In silence, the duo was dribbling the obstacles of the path with never daunted force. They seemed to never tire and be in complete ecstasy. As he approached the designated point, he changed the direction of the look, pointing to something, stating: "This is the place that was in my dream last night." A kind of happiness filled the heart with that little fisherman reaffirming what he believed in, Mary was there. That was a day that would come into the story. Satisfied, prayed a little, and then they left to take care of their respective obligations. There was a lot to do for Mary's work.

The fourth appearance

It was the beginning of September month. Along with friends, the psychic returned to the point of appearances. As soon as they arrived at the scene, Rosario was prayed. At the end of this religious exercise, they could clearly see lightning. In a row, there was another one. That's when the Immaculate Conception appeared in the cloud under a small tree. See how the psychic describes her: "She was dressed in a pale cream-colored robe. He had no veil, no crown, no cloak. No adornment or embroidery. The dress was long, with long sleeves, and it had a pink string on its waist. His hair fell to his shoulders and it was brown. The eyes too, though much clearer, almost the color of honey. All of it radiated light. She looked like you, but she was a child. That's where the contact was initiated.

"What do you want?

"I want you to pray for Rosario.

"Allow yourself to be seen so that everyone will believe. These people who are here want to see you.

"No. It's enough that you give them the message because for those who believe it will be enough, and for those who don't believe it, even if he sees me, he won't believe it.

"We were thinking of building a church in your honor. What do you say to that?

"No. The Lord doesn't want material churches. He wants living temples, which are yourselves. Restore the holy temple of the Lord. In you is the satisfaction of the Lord.

"I wish to improve as a human being. What values are essential?

"Love each other. Love each other. Forgive each other. Make peace. Don't ask for her first.

"What do I do with the money they gave me?

"Make a donation to a chapel in Cuapa. From this day forward, don't take a penny for nothing.

"Where can we go to communion with God?

"In themselves. The Church is yourselves. The material things are called prayer houses.

"Should I continue in the catechumenate?

"No. Don't let him. Always stay strong in the catechumenate. Little by little you'll understand everything the catechumenate means. Like a community group meditate on the beatitudes, away from all the noise.

"When should I come back here?

"On October 13th.

That said, the cloud has risen by taking with you to the saint. The group said goodbye to the site starting their return to their respective homes. They would fulfill the absent obligations with the certainty that they were blessed by the mother of God. Long live the Holy Mother of God!

The fifth appearance

On the 8th, the devoted Marians attended the site of appearances paying their master's honor. As you knew, the virgin didn't show up, but that's why they didn't stop enjoying their contact with nature learning more about the divine. After a long time, they returned to their homes promising to return another day.

The occasion was given on the 13th, where people attended after everyday devotion in the chapel. At the scene, the Rosario began and praise God. In the third mystery, there is the formation of a bright circle on the floor. The light came from the sky and directing the look up, saw it as if it was a bright ring floating over them. What a thrill the people present!

It didn't take long and followed the phenomenon of lightning. Our Lady then introduced herself to the psychic landing manly on the flowers brought by the pilgrims.

Our Lady is in the pile of rocks about the flowers, warned the psychic.

"People have fixed their eyes in the right direction. Some have seen and some not, what made the shepherd a little upset.

"Bless you, my mother! Could you show yourself to the others?

"No! Not everyone can see me!

"Not satisfied with the answer, the fisherman insisted.

"Madam, allow them to see you, so they can believe you! Because many don't believe it. They tell me it's the demon that comes to me. And that the virgin is dead and returned to dust like any mortal. Allow them to see you, Holy Mother!

The Queen of Heaven's reaction was instantaneous, raised her hands to her chest, pale, her robe became gray and her expression became sad and dissolute. Tears started rolling from your face like it was a distress call. In that, your servant took the initiative.

"Madam, forgive me for what I told you! I'm guilty! The lady's mad at me. Forgive me! Forgive me!

"I'm not mad or angry.

"Why are you crying? I see her crying.

"I'm sorry to see the hard of these people's hearts. But you'll have to pray for them that they change.

This response has the power of a devastating earthquake destabilizing the employee's emotions. It caused a compulsive cry on him. Among this whirlwind of emotions, the saint continued to pass the messages.

"Pray the Rosario, meditate the mysteries. Hear the Word of God that lies in them. Love each other. Love each other. Forgive each other. Make peace. Don't ask for peace without making peace because if you don't do it, it's not good to ask for it. Do your duty. Put the word of God into practice. Find ways to please God. Serve your next one because that way you will please him.

"Ma'am, I have many orders, but I forgot about them. There are many. The lady knows all of them.

"They ask me for things that aren't relevant. Ask for faith that they have the strength so that each one can carry their cross. The sufferings of this world cannot be suppressed. The suffering is the cross you must bear. That's life. There's trouble with the husband, with the wife, with the kids, with the brothers. Talk, talk, talk, talk, and make peace. Don't go back to violence. Never return to violence. Pray for faith that you will be patient.

"I got it. Each must accept his cross!

"You won't see me in this place anymore.

"Don't leave us, my mother.

"Don't be upset. I'm with you, although you can't see me. I am the mother of all of you sinners. Love each other. Forgive yourselves. Make peace because if you don't, there'll be no peace. Don't go back to violence. Never turn to violence. Nicaragua has suffered a lot since the earthquake and will continue to suffer if you all don't change. If you don't change, you'll rush the beginning of World War III. Pray, pray, my son, all over the world. A mother never forgets her children. And I haven't forgotten what you've suffered.

That said, it has gradually raised to the heavens. It will be as marked as the certainty that the Lady would never abandon them as she promised herself. Thank you and praise the virgin of heaven.

Our Lady Queen and messenger of peace

Jacareí-Brazil (1991-2017)

Jacareí is located 100 kilometers from São Paulo. The access road to the site is through the BR 116, a stretch that links São Paulo to Rio de Janeiro.

The city is consecrated to Our Immaculate Conception before even the official proclamation of the dogma of the Immaculate Conception. By divine providence, she was chosen to be the headquarters of important appearances of the heavenly forces. Bless our mother!

Main messages in Jacareí

My son, my son! You have to sanctify yourself. Holiness is a difficult path, but... its end is real and glorious.

I come to ask prayers done with love. Prayer that leads men to understand love.

Concentrate on prayer, live with humility.

I wish you to love me more and more, to offer me your heart more and more. Love the God of all things, always forgive and increasingly your offenders.

Give me more and more heart... Tell my children to continue praying with love and trust; don't lose hope in God!

Look at my heart, surrounded by thorns and pain... I take in my heart your sufferings; I offer them to the Lord in my heart.

Keep praying the Holy Third... He is my favorite prayer, is the current that you will hold Satan with, and renew the face of the whole world!

I ask you to love each other. Go to the Eucharist Table to receive the Eternal Food!

Third must be accompanied by regret! Let there be contrition in the heart!

My children, I wish you, my peace! Pray! Pray! Ask forgiveness for the sinners.

Pray with your heart! Open up to God and his love! Live happy and peace fill your lives.

Plant the peace on yourselves, and diffuse the others this peace. I love them and I want to give them my Heaven Peace! I bless you.

Pray and live peace in their hearts. Plant it in your hearts and live with love. When you feel confused, pray, ask for the Light of the Holy Spirit, read the Gospel, and it will all be clear.

If you want to make me happy, pray continuously for the poor sinners.

I also pray to my son Jesus so that you grant me the thanks necessary to help them! Follow my example, and pray too.

You can't reach it, unless you pray! And when you ask them, ask them whenever the will of God is done, not your will.

Satan is loose in the world, looking to drag all souls into sin and conviction. The only defense of Christians against him is with a lot of prayer and fast.

I'm crying because the sins of the world are too big, and because my requests are not answered. Many souls are condemning themselves and a great punishment will fall on the face of the earth... Pray a lot!

Our Immaculate Lady Appeared Conception

Brazil Reserve-1995

Elizete, Juliano, Janaina and Alice were four students from the countryside. Every day, a couple of students moved into a source where they were going to wash the dishes of the lunch. On one of these occasions, young Elizete was surprised to see a gorgeous light, and it came out a man. Seeing the girl was scared, he reassured her:

"Don't be afraid! My name is Gabriel, the angel of peace. Come back here in three days, and you'll have a surprise. Don't tell anyone about this!

"I get it! Okay!

The angel disappeared, and the young lady went back to school on her way to finish the day class. As agreed, she returned to the specified date. You saw the light again, only in the shape of Our Lady appeared. Curious, tried to touch the image. That she moved! Scared, he walked away. That's when he heard:

"Don't be afraid! I am the mother of heaven, the mother of Jesus.

Still, you didn't have the guts to come back. From that day on, she started acting strangely, what caught her teacher's attention. Trust her as a friend, she revealed the secret and from then some young people would gather around and pray at the site of the appearances.

A series of visions began where the Queen of Heaven has presented itself to many people.

Main messages on the reserve

"Dear children don't watch soap operas, horror shows, movies, and drawings. Watch out. The enemy has many plans to destroy families, and it makes me sorrowful. I love you guys so much. Don't follow fashion. Pray for those who only think of the things of this world. Bless you all. Amen.

"Jesus is happy with people who pray, have faith and ask. I invite you to be with me in heaven one day, God's address. My children, for my Son Jesus, I thank you for all who pray to Rosario in this place, and I ask you to pray for those who do not pray. Only the Holy Spirit will light you up to get closer and closer to God. My children, when Jesus returns wants to avoid finding his children in vices, renounce smoke, alcohol, and drugs. It is for prayer that you will be released. Jesus wants to save everyone from sin, he died on the cross to save everyone and continues to heal and freed from all evil. I thank you and bless you all. Amen.

"Dear children, the return of my son Jesus is very close, when he returns that his children are prepared, not sleeping in faith. Children, Jesus will spill the Holy Spirit upon you. Pray and pray. Beware of Satan, so I don't destroy my plans. Always keep your heart open for Jesus to come in. Amen.

"My dear children, I pray once more to Rosario, Satan does not come near those who pray with me. Be strong, I will always be with you in the ordeals. Bless you. Amen.

"Kids listen to their parents. My children, at the end my heart will triumph. Pray, pray. Amen

"Pray for those who ask for prayers, for the children of the street and for the sick, I will bless you all. Pray, pray, this is my request.

"My dear daughter goes to Sunday school every day at mass, you'll always have my protection. I thank all the people who prayed yesterday a thousand Hail Mary. Thank you for the sacrifices, prayers they've done and offered for me and my son Jesus. For all my mother blessing and illumination of the Holy Spirit. Amen.

"Dear children, the Holy Heart of Jesus is the source of all love. Pray and consecrate each day to His Heart. Amen.

"Dear children, I am the Queen of Peace, the mother of all of you. Hurry, hurry, pray for the conversion of sinners. I wish peace for all. Amen.

"Son, I came to the earth to ask you to pray, and to teach you all to pray especially the Rosario that is my simple prayer. My love for you is so great. Bless you. Amen.

"My dear brothers took my mother in, took me in. Mine will take it with me one day. Amen.

"Dear children, I ask prayer, penance and fasting for the conversion of young people." Amen. I give you, my peace.

"Dear children, be always happy, Jesus is always with you in the ordeals. Be obedient and pray. Children pray in this carnival time, my children hurt my heart and the heart of my son Jesus. In these days, pray a thousand Hail Mary in repair of sins committed. Amen.

"My dear children, I wish you peace. Live in charity and love. Love is the light of conversion. Children, Jesus is the path of light, I wish that everyone save themselves from sin. Pray, children.

"Today again I invite you all to conversion, do penance, prayers, and fast on Wednesdays and Fridays. I chose you children for you to ask, "Pray, pray, pray."

"My dear children, I'm coming from heaven to earth to save my children. I am the patron of your Brazil, your Immaculate Mother of Peace Conception.

"Little brother, my love is so great for you. I wish each one my peace, my love. I spill in their hearts my peace. Amen.

"My dear children, I invite you to accept peace and pray for peace. Amen.

"Dear children, Jesus is the light of the world. Live in charity and forgiveness. Does everything I ask you and be saint as thy Father of Heaven is holy? Amen.

"Be like children in my lap. Love God, love the next and forgive yourself as brothers. On this special day, I want to ask you to hurry in the conversion. Do penance, fasts, and prayers. Jesus' return is near. Bless you. Amen.

"My dear children, I am in the middle of you, I ask you to pray for Papa John Paul II, for the Bishop and the Priests. I'll give peace to everyone. Amen.

"Dear children, pray, pray, pray." *Jesus died on the cross for sinners. Meditate about Jesus' suffering and death for us. I bless you. Amen.*

"Dear children, I cry tears of blood for my children to convert, yet many do not accept conversion. So, beloved children, pray and pray for the conversion of sinners, for the hard hearts of stone. Amen. Amen.

"Kids, today I invite you to kneel at the feet of my son Jesus who is in the tabernacle and worship you. Love it, love it. Amen.

"My dear children, I am in the middle of you and I invite you to pray more and more. Don't get discouraged in the ordeals. I'll give them strength. Bless you all.

"Dear children, I come here today to bring my peace. Pray for those who criticize them, those who don't accept me. I am the mother of all, delivered by my son Jesus. Bless you all. Amen.

"My dear children, today I ask you to pray for families, for the consecrated to my heart.

"Dear brothers, you are living in a Thanksgiving and many tribulations. Pray. Bless you. Amen.

"My dear children, I ask you to convert to my son Jesus. Love to your next. Do as I ask. I love you all. Amen.

"Dear little brothers, the peace of our Lord Jesus Christ be with you. I will always be with you, in all dangers pray with me and fear not, believe only. I am the angel of peace; my name is Gabriel Archangel.

"Peace be with you. Dear little children, have faith alive and true. Only your prayers will help these days you're living. I love them very much and don't get discouraged. Pray all the time. Bless you. Amen.

"Dear children, consecrate my Immaculate Heart and my son, Jesus. I'm rushing to convert. When you praise me and my son, angels party in heaven. I love you all and bless you. Amen.

"Dear brothers convert, convert, for times are brief." I love you all and bless you for the Holy Trinity. Father, Son and Holy Spirit. Amen.

"My son Jesus and my love are always in their hearts. Every day I stand beside you, I see you praying, working, I'm the mother of Love. So welcome in your hearts, my mother's love. I'm pleased with the people who are praying and converting. I appreciate the flowers you bring me. Take my graces and blessings. Never forget I love you so much. Amen.

"My children, I cry for my children who don't care about God. I always intercept Jesus for all my children. I'll take it back until the day of punishment my children convert. Furthermore, I'll have my messengers transmit my messages. Children, I need your prayers, sacrifices, to help me.

"My dear children, today again I ask for conversion and pray more because in today's world many want to know more than God. Many of my children are getting lost, to exchange the true Church of Jesus Christ, for false religions and cults. I ask you to pray for the priests, for the bishops not to be discouraged on the hike.

"My brothers, I am the living and true God, believe in Eucharist. I'm present and I'm Jesus himself. I give my peace to everyone. Amen.

"Many kids here are hurting my Immaculate Heart. I love everyone with motherly love. I ask you to convert, for times are approaching. Go to masses. Pray for the souls of purgatory. When I cry, hell jumps with joy. As in Heaven, Mother welcomes everyone into my heart. Don't think the evil one is sleeping, he's every moment wanting to take over you. Pray to help me close the doors of hell. Many, many children don't believe in Eucharistic anymore. Believe me, Jesus while you can receive in your hearts in communion, for when the false pope sits in the chair, he forbids Eucharistic and confession and many other things. Help me. Amen. Amen.

"Dear children, it is with joy that I transmit this message. Jesus is asking you to pray, to convert, Jesus is rushing, for His return is near. Pray for the Holy Father, Papa John Paul II, that he has strength and faith in this walk. I, Mother of Jesus, bless you for the Holy Trinity. Father, Son and Holy Spirit. Amen.

"I bring you this message with lots of love and joy. Pray the Holy Rosario with faith, love, and devotion. Give God your hearts. He hears your prayers. Jesus wants to be worshiped in the Holy Sacramento. I bless you for the Holy Trinity, Father, Son and Holy Spirit. Amen.

"My dear children, today I come down from heaven to bless you. I am the Immaculate Conception of the Queen of Peace, and I want to ask you to consecrate the Holy Heart of Jesus and my "Immaculate Heart. I've filled your hearts with peace and joy. Furthermore, I'm happy with you because I love you all with motherly love. I bless you all for the Holy Trinity. Amen. I appreciate you corresponding to my appeal.

"My dear children, today my son Jesus was born to save them from sin. Many on that day don't even remember that God exists. They only think of parties, fun, and they don't even remember praying the Third, because they only think about the things in the world, so I ask you to convert to win the sky. We the Holy Family bless you all. Amen. Father, Son and Holy Spirit.

"Dear children, peace be in their hearts. Today, I come down from heaven to ask you to convert as soon as Jesus' return is near.

"Dear children, today it is with much love that I give this message. I love you very much, and I ask you not to discourage this walk, I am with you and bless you, for the Father, Son and Holy Spirit. Amen. My children, I ask you to pray to Rosario every day because he ties Satan. I'm always with you. Amen.

"My beloved children are approaching punishment. They become as soon as possible because otherwise they will go into eternal fire. Convert. I want to take them with me to heaven. Oh children, how I cry for those who don't believe, and don't care about God. I love you both so much and bless you. Amen.

"Kids are with great joy that I'm here today to ask you to do more work on prayers, to fast on Wednesdays and Fridays, to do penance for this work. Be careful of the enemy because these days there will be plenty of ordeals. I'll always be with you. Bless you. Amen.

"The peace of my son Jesus and my peace remain with you. Sons, I thank you for raising this cross as a sign of my victory, and the defeat of Satan. Me and my son Jesus, we were present helping them. After you cease my appearances, I ask you to continue with the devotion of the first Friday of the month in disagreement to the Holy Heart of Jesus, the first Saturday of the month dedicated to my Immaculate Heart and the first Saturday of the month dedicated to my Immaculate Heart and the first Sunday dedicated to both hearts, Jesus and Mary's first Saturday of the month of the Holy

Heart of Jesus, the first Saturday of the month dedicated to my Immaculate Heart and the first Sunday dedicated to both hearts, Jesus and Mary's first Saturday of the month of the Holy Heart of Jesus, the first Saturday of the month dedicated to my I'm going to I want this place to be turned into a little Medjugorje. Bless you. Amen.

"Dear sons come down from heaven to tell you, I want you to keep praying every day, here in my cave and keep living my messages. They're taking you, my children, to the path of heaven. I don't want you to abandon what Jesus and I have taught you. My children, one day you will pay for this, so pray and seek to live what we taught you. Sons, I thank all those who are here helping us with this work. I want you to keep going and don't stop. Jesus and I thank you for everything. I leave my blessing to all of you. Amen.

"My children, I want to welcome you today to all of you in my Immaculate Heart, and in the heart of my son Jesus. Kids, don't forget to keep coming here so simple, I chose to give my messages. All consecrated to our hearts are guarded in my Immaculate "Heart and the Holy Heart of my son Jesus. Today I come with joy and lots of love to give you this message. Don't forget, always pray to Rosario with devotion. I thank you, my dear children, for being together another day, praised to my heart and to my son Jesus. Today I shall pour many thanks upon all of you, my beloved. Keep doing fasts and penance, always go to Holy Mass, commune and confess. Enjoy it because times are short. I am the Peace Queen. Don't get discouraged. Live my messages and not only listen to them. My love for you is endless. Believe my signs here. I will no longer be with you physically visible, but I will always be with you at every moment of your lives. I'm pleased with you, so I cry with joy. Furthermore, I bless you for the Father, the Son and the Holy Spirit. Amen.

"My children, my generation, today I come to announce you with love my messages for your conversion. My beloved brothers, people listen to me

carefully this message and keep putting it into practice. Enjoy this time to welcome me, with love, in Eucharist. I love them and ask them to pray Rosario as a family. Make fasts and repairing penitence, for many men and women are sinning against my most holy Heart. I don't want men to behave like women and women like their men. Take this urgent request because I love you very much. My glorious coming is very close. I leave my blessing. Amen.

Special chapter

Our Lady has always accompanied me on my path over the earth. Mother and counselor, objectifies my good at all costs and that's what she wants for her life. Down there, follows some of my spiritual experiences and dates with the mother of God.

Under a tree

It was almost noon. Despite the heat, the environment was quiet and cozy to be among the trees of the garden of a square. I was thinking about life and the difficulties when suddenly a beautiful, strong, old woman came to me. Smiling, she questioned:

"Do you believe in God, my son?

"Yes, I do.

So, without asking permission, she put her right hand on my forehead praying:

"May the power and glory of the creator cover you and light you up.

At this very moment, I felt a deep peace and joy. It was like I felt complete. Instants later, the lady said goodbye to me gently. I followed her a little until no explanation disappeared from my vision. I tried to look for her, but unsuccessfully. It just evaporated. I have bewitched this presence to the mother of God as a vow of faith.

In the lottery house

I was playing some games to try my luck like any ordinary citizen. In line, before I did, and there was a figure of a mulatto woman dressed in franchises. She stared at me and asked:

"Can you help me, young man, with a few bucks?

"Our looks changed in her feeling a complete confidence. Smiling, I said: "Yes. I can!

I gave him some coins out of my pocket. Thanks, she just stood there trying her luck. I approached the attendance window and paid my bill. When I left, I couldn't see my benefactor anymore. Asking some gifts about her, they simply said they didn't see such a woman. In my intimate, my heart just pounded! Did…! There was no doubt that it was God's mother testing my goodness, and thank God I corresponded to your expectations.

In the crowd

It was a day like any other. I was inside the crowd hoping to arrive more passengers when a beautiful lady arrived. She sat next to me and opened a nice smile. I felt intimately connected to that stranger with no real explanation. It seemed like we'd known each other a long time. Without power, resisting, I initiated contact:

"Everything okay, ma'am?

"I'm fine. How are you?

"Living life. What's your name, and where do you live?

"My name is Mary and I live in Belo Garden. I'm married and I have three children.

"Good! My name is Aldivan and I'm next door. I live with my mother and brothers.

"Do you still have a mother? That's good. I've already lost my mother. It's so sad. Mom is the most important thing in our life, isn't it?

"Yes. Mothers never die. They're always with us, one way or another.

"Now that you've told me that, I get emotional! You mean I'll find my mother again after I die?

"Before and after.

"Good! You have a child's soul. He must be a good boy!

"With my work, I help ten people directly and thousands indirectly through public service. I feel fulfilled.

"How wonderful!

"What's your religion?

"I'm Catholic. One of my children is a carpenter, father's trade. We're a very close family, you know? I have a project and through it, I help many people.

"How cool! I'd also like to join a project like that. But occasionally, there's time.

"Don't talk like that! Sometimes just one word is enough to help the next.

"I get it. I don't know how, but I feel very comfortable with you.

"Good! Me too! Must be because light attracts light, doesn't it?

"Yes!

"Look! I loved meeting you! I know that sometime your dreams will be fulfilled. You're an excellent boy!

"I loved meeting you too!

"Thank you!

The car leaves, and we keep quiet during the course. When I said goodbye to her, it was a trail of longing. I found that woman a true face of Mary. A real mother! Long live the Holy Mother of God!

Personal miracles

I've got two miracles through the intercession of Our Lady, one respiratory problem and another vascular. Both times, I felt the hand of God healing me, which moved me very much. My example is proof that everyone believes in the love of God and his mother for humanity. Long live Mary!

Message received when I started writing the book

"I'm pleased with your decision. I'll protect you and give you plenty of peace!"

Here I bid farewell after this wonderful report with the certainty of the mission accomplished. May God's mother's name be more and more and more!

The end

www.ingramcontent.com/pod-product-compliance
Lightning Source LLC
LaVergne TN
LVHW020440080526
838202LV00055B/5289